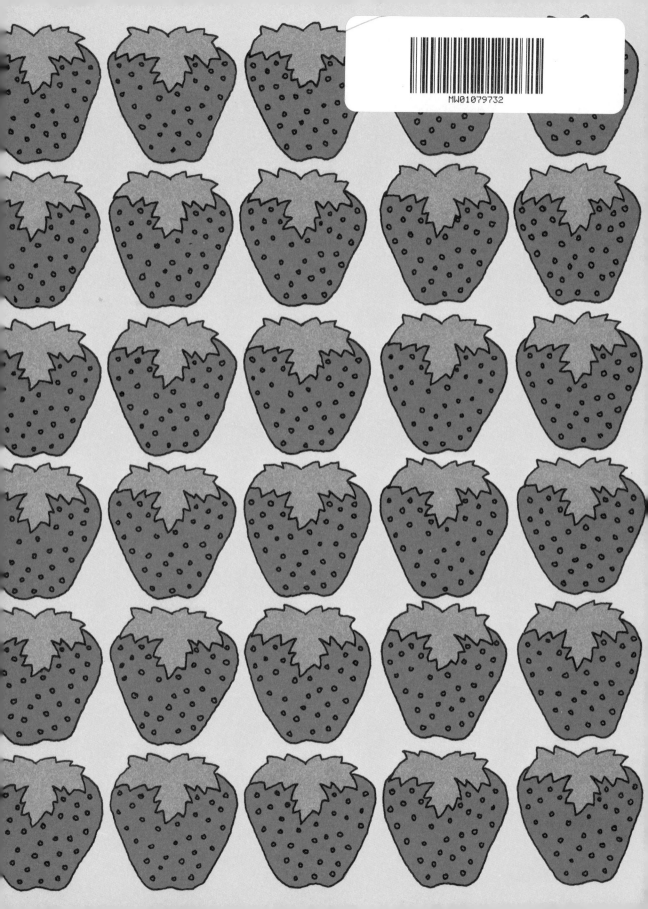

MW01079732

this
strawberry book
belongs to

*this book
is for
Jane
and
Bruno*

Weekly Reader Books Edition

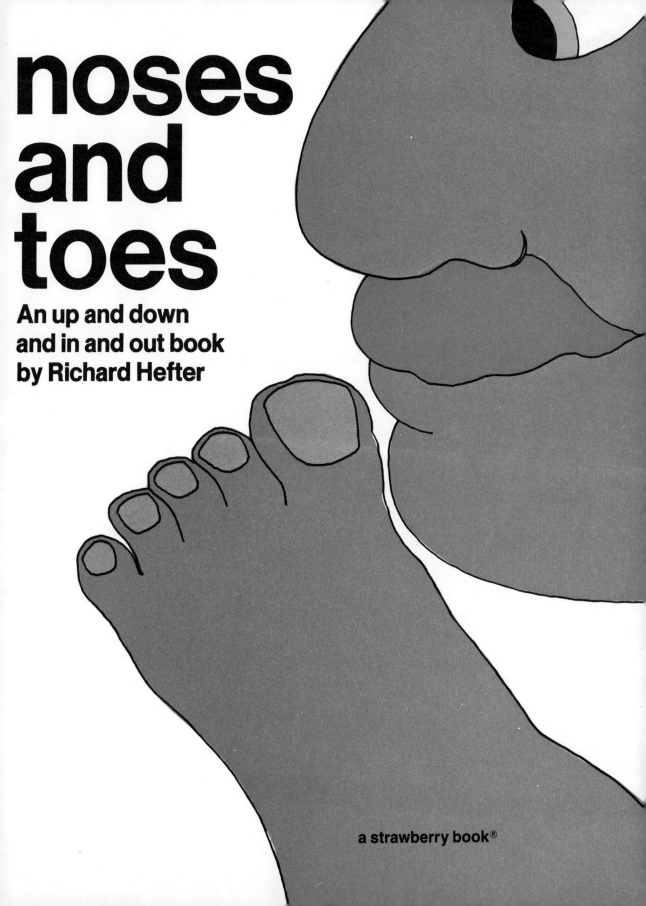

noses
and
toes

**An up and down
and in and out book
by Richard Hefter**

a strawberry book®

Nose up
Toes down

Pears on bears

Bears in chairs

**Pairs of bears with chairs
going up the stairs**

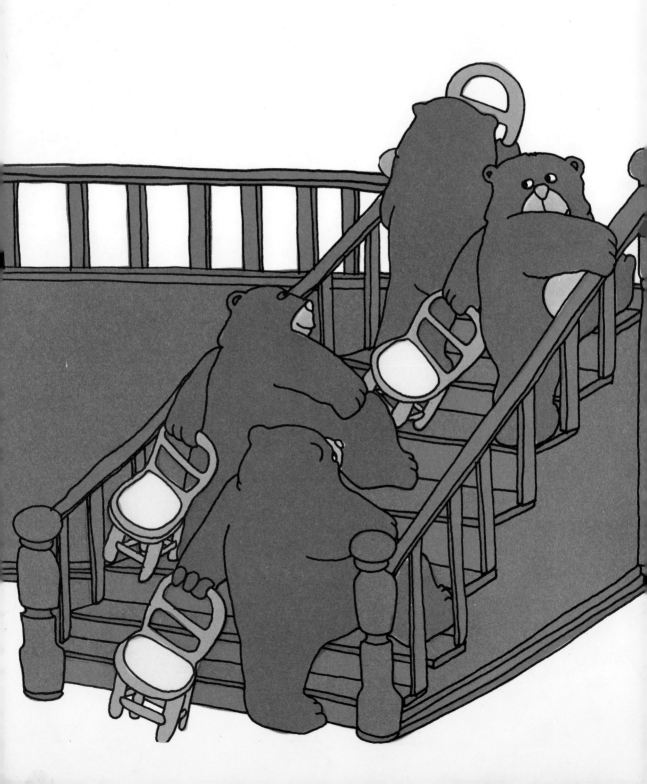

Hairy pairs of bears
running down the stairs

and out the door

A fox in a box

A fox wearing socks

A fox on a box
full of locks,
rocks and clocks

Nose and toes in roses.

Roses in nose and toes.

Rows and rows
of toes and roses

Rabbits on elephants

Elephants on rabbits

Tired rabbits under elephants

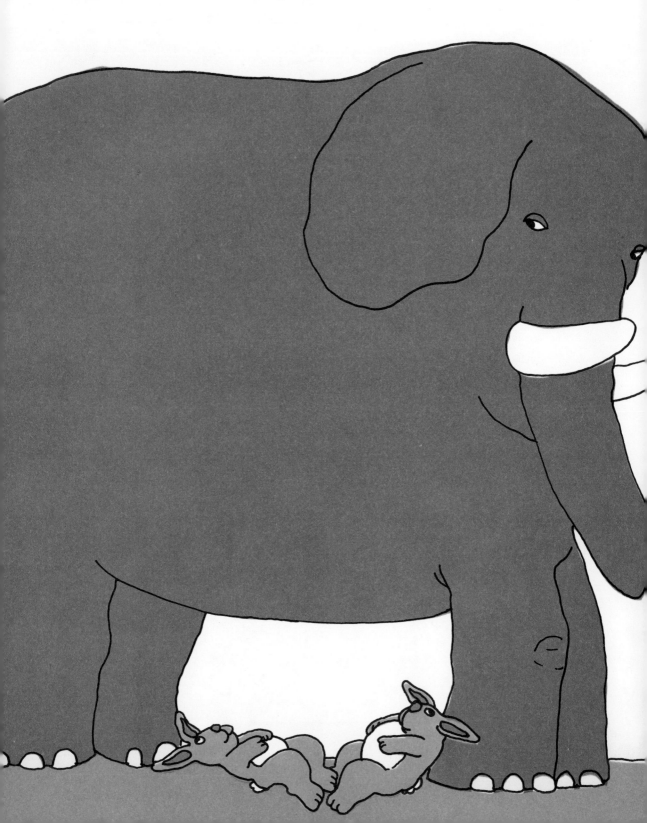

resting

Mouse in cheese

Cheese in mouse

Mouse in house

goodbye house mouse

Yaks in sacks

Axes and packs on backs of yaks

A pack of yaks in slacks

Playing jacks

While Max yak
with a pack on his back
hikes to Hackensack

...and back